"CATS AND DOGS"

MUTTS II
by
· PATRICK McDONNELL ·

Andrews McMeel
Publishing

Kansas City

Mutts is distributed internationally by King Features Syndicate, Inc. For information write King Features Syndicate, Inc., 216 East 45th Street, New York, New York 10017.

www.andrewsmcmeel.com

ISBN: 0-8362-3732-3

Library of Congress Catalog Card Number: 97-71625

Mutts Too, Also is printed on recycled paper.

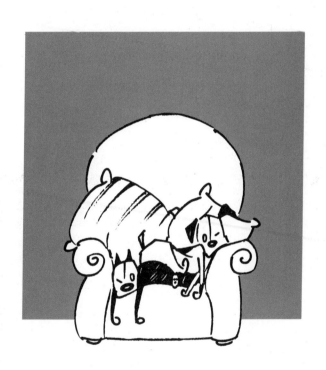

22

24

WOOF! ROWF!

HEY, GUARD DOG, WHY ARE YOU ALWAYS ON EDGE?

IT'S NERVES... IT'S TEMPERAMENT... IT'S **DISPOSITION!**

YOU OUGHTA TRY DIS POSITION.

I'M TELLING YOU, GUARD DOG, YOU'RE **TOO** HIGH STRUNG. YOU **MUST** LEARN TO RELAX.

YESH.

RELAX!?! I'M A GUARD DOG! I FLIRT WITH **FEAR!!!** GRRR I DANCE WITH **DANGER!!!!!** **WHO** THE **HECK** CAN **RELAX** WHEN THEY'RE **FACE** TO **FACE** WITH **RAGING TERROR!?!**

Z-Z-Z-Z

! !

SO, **MOOCH** HERE IS GOING TO TEACH **ME** HOW TO RELAX?

YESH.

US CATS HAVE **LONG** MASTERED THE ANCIENT ARTS OF MEDITATION. ...FIRST YOU MUST **CLEAR** THE MIND OF **ALL** THOUGHT.

THUSLY...

YEH YEH WHAT'S **NEXT!?!**

I CAN'T THINK.

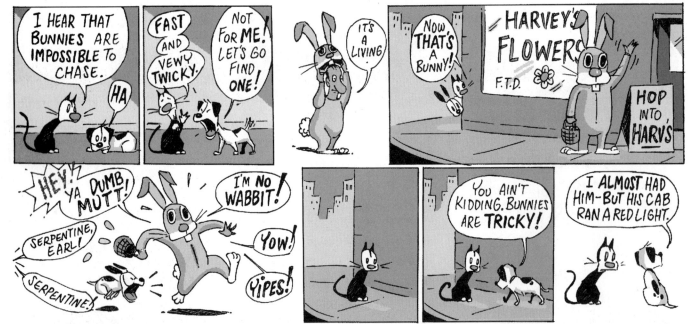

OH, MUMSHY...DEVOTED, LOVING **MAW!** SHE WHO CARRIED ME BY THE SHCRUFF OF MY WITTLE NECK; **SHE** WHO LICKED MY DIRTY WITTLE FACE; **SHE** WHO PURRED ME TO SHWEET, SHWEET SLEEP...

MOOCH! WHAT HAPPENED!?! WERE YOU HIT BY A TRUCK!

CLOSE...

... I'M IN LOVE!

EARL, I'M TELLIN' YA—I'M IN LOVE! YESH, LOVE!!!

WITH A SHWELL HOUSE CAT NAMED SHNELLY... SHWEET, SHWEET, SHWEET SHNELLY!

AHHHHHH

THERE GOES ONE SHMITTEN KITTEN.

WELL, I'M OFF TO SEE MY SHNELLY! SHE'S A HOUSE CAT, YOU KNOW, CONFINED TO HER ABODE, YOU KNOW, IT'S UP TO ME, A CAT OF THE WORLD, TO SHWEEP HER OFF HER FEETS, YOU KNOW.

WHAT'S THAT SMELL!?! I DABBED A LITTLE SARDINE BEHIND MY EARS.

WHO LET YOU OUT OF THE HOUSE!?!

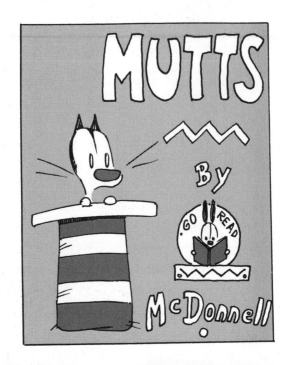

SUCH A PITY... LOCKED INDOORS, NEVER TO FEEL THE TENDER CARESS OF GOOD OL' MOTHER NATURE WITH ALL HER WARM CHARMS AND MAGNIFICENT

MOOD SWINGS

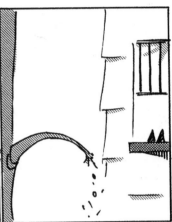

WHAT HAPPENED?

YOU FELL OUT OF THE TREE AGAIN.

OH, YEH... I GOT "BONKY ON THE KONKY"... **BUT**, HOW DID I WIND UP HOME IN BED!?!

I CARRIED YOU.

THANKS, PAL.

S'OKAY... I ALWAYS LIKE TO SHOW KINDNESS TO DUMB ANIMALS.

PLEASE **FLY** TO MY SHNELLY AND GIVE HER MY **LOVE**.

FLY, MY FRIEND, FLY TO MY SHNELLY!

I WISH I HAD WINGS

... AND TWO DRUMSTICKS WITH GRAVY.

A **CACTUS** FOR SHNELLY. STUCK IN HER HOUSE - SHE NEVER GETS TO SEE ANYTHING **DIFFERENT**.

YOW YIPES OOPS!

WELL **THAT** WAS CERTAINLY DIFFER- ENT.

NAH, SAME THING HAPPENED YESTERDAY.

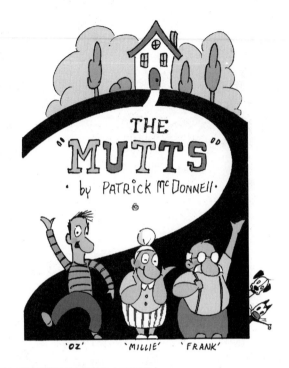

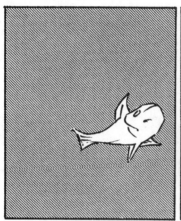

by
Patrick
Mc
Donnell

I WISH HE COULD **HOLD** ON TO THIS **THING**.

DO YOU THINK THE WORLD IS **FLAT**, MOOCH!

I DUNNO...

I FIND IT KIND OF **LUMPY**.

HOWMPF DOSH ITAAS?

BITTY CHOOF FEE.

AWL TAY!

YESHX

ALL RIGHT! **WHO** ATE **ALL** THE SALTWATER TAFFY?

WOW! ISN'T IT GREAT HOW **TRAVEL** CAN REALLY **BROADEN** ONE'S VIEW OF THE **WORLD**?!!

HEY! I CAN SEE MYSELF IN THE **WATER!**

WOW!

THAT'S THE BIGGEST **FISH** I EVER SAW!

HEY! I'M A **MAMMAL** JUST LIKE **YOU!**

BIG... AND SHTUPID.

YOU, DOLLFISH, SURE **TALK** FUNNY.

WE COMMUNICATE WITH A SERIES OF WHISTLES.

WHAT D'YA KNOW! MY OZZIE CAN SPEAK FLUENT DOLPHINESE!

MY OZZIE'S PACKING. I GUESS **WE** ARE GOING **HOME.**

BUT **I** DON'T WANT TO GO **HOME!** I LIKE BEING ON VACATION AND DOING **NOTHING!**

BUT YOU DO "**NOTHING**" AT **HOME!**

YESH.

BUT HERE **I** DO IT IN **STYLE.**

YA KNOW, MOOCH, THE HARDEST PART OF ENDING A VACATION IS LEAVING **ALL** YOUR NEWFOUND FRIENDS

SKRITCH SKRATCH SKRATCH,

AND **THEY** YOU.

SAY GOODBYE TO THE OCEAN!

BYE.

GEE, OZZIE, YOUR EARL SURE **LIKES** CAR RIDES.

WHAT ABOUT MOOCH?

HE'S GETTING BETTER.

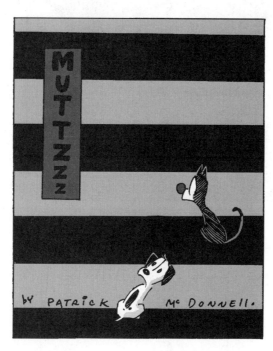

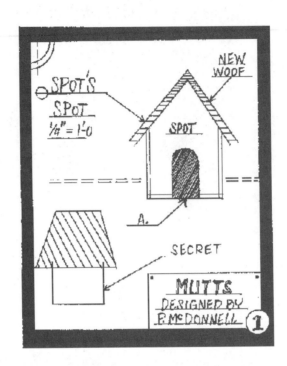

'DOG SHOW'

So, HARRY...

How DO YOU GET A PRIZE AROUND THIS JOINT!?! ATHLETIC SKILLS? CIRCUS TRICKS? BRAINTEASERS?

NO, WE'RE SOLELY JUDGED ON OUR BEAUTY.

YIKES! HOW CAN ANYONE WIN!?! THEY'RE ALL DOGS!

!?!

ALL RIGHT! WHO'S NEXT FOR THEIR DOG SHOW GROOMING?

OKAY, FIDO. YOU'RE IT!

AND, BROTHER, YOU ARE THE FUNNIEST-LOOKING MUTT TODAY.

!

RZZZZZZ

IF YOU ASK ME

...ALL OF THIS IN-BREEDING HAS GOTTEN OUT OF HAND!

WELL...

BOYS, I NOW HAVE A NEW HAIRCUT AND A NUMBER. HECK, I THINK I CAN WIN THIS DOG SHOW THING!

I JUST DON'T KNOW MY CATEGORY...

CERTIFIABLE.

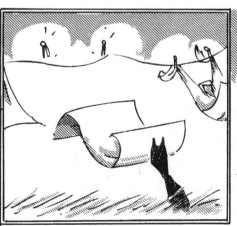

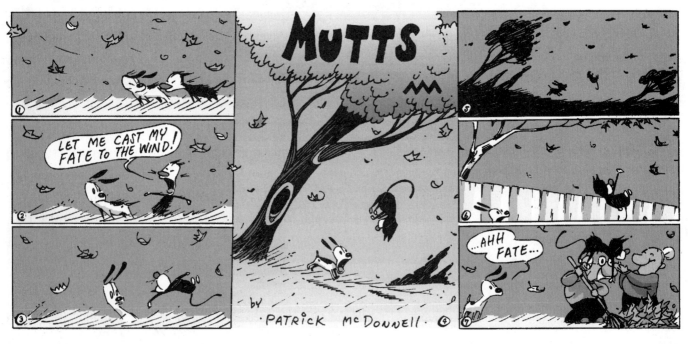

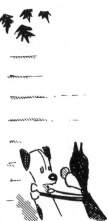

107

YOU SHOULD GO BACK TO YOUR WIFE... WHO ELSE WOULD LIVE WITH A CRAB?

YES... SHE'S A SAINT.

KNOCK KNOCK

WHO'S THERE?

G☆#!!

WHO?

"THE OLD LADY."

LOLLIPOP!

I AIN'T SO OLD.

AHH, YESH...

FORGIVES ME, LOLLIPOP, I LOVES YA!

LIKEWISE, CRABCAKES

AHH, THE MIRACLE OF MARRIAGE. A BOND OF **LOVE**... SO SHTRONG... YET SO FRAGILE... HOW DOES IT SHURVIVE?

G☆#!!

A HARD SHELL HELPS.

WHAT HAPPENED TO YOUR **NOSE**!?!

AAH, CRABBY AND HIS WIFE LOLLIPOP KEPT **PINCHING** IT! THANK GOODNESS THEY LEFT YESHTERDAY!

A·HA! THAT SLIPPERY MOOCH! SNEAKING OUT AT NIGHT! HOW CAN ANYONE BE SO SECRETIVE? SO SLY? SO SHIFTY?

I BETTER SHADOW HIM.

OH NO! MOOCH MIGHT BE INVOLVED WITH DANGEROUS NIGHT CREATURES LIKE SKUNKS! OR RACCOONS! OR

CATS!

...THE WORST KIND!

IT'S TWO O'CLOCK

BARK BARK BARK

SHADDUP!

ARF! ARF MEOW ARF

AND ALL'S WELL.

111

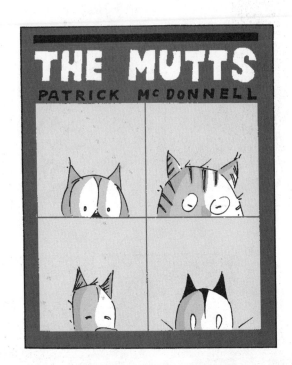

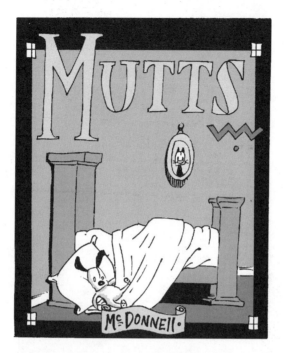

MOOCH!!! NOW WE'RE **ALL** LOST!

No! YOUR DOGGY NOSE CAN **SHNIFF** OUR WAY BACK!

SHMAYBE SOMEONE WILL SAVE US...

HUH!?! WHAT OTHER **NUT** WOULD BE OUT ON A NIGHT LIKE THIS!?!

HELLO, BOYS...

YELLO.

I DO **HOPE** IT'S MY **KITTY** YOU FOUND. DESPITE **ALL** MY WEALTH, IT IS THE ONLY GIFT MY PRECIOUS DAUGHTER **PRAYS** FOR.

WELL, I'M SURE YOU KNOW, MR. GREY—"MONEY **CAN'T BUY** LOVE."

ON THE CONTRARY.

ONE CAN PURCHASE "UNCONDITIONAL" LOVE AT ANY ANIMAL SHELTER FOR A SMALL FEE!